To:

From:

Benjamin
FRANKLIN

Wit
AND
Wisdom

PETER PAUPER PRESS, INC.
WHITE PLAINS, NEW YORK

Photos on jacket and title page
from Corbis-Bettmann,
902 Broadway, New York, NY 10010

Copyright © 1998
Peter Pauper Press, Inc.
202 Mamaroneck Avenue
White Plains, NY 10601
All rights reserved
ISBN 978-0-88088-081-7
Printed in China
28 27 26 25 24

Benjamin Franklin
Wit and Wisdom

The wise sayings which follow
come from many different numbers
of Ben Franklin's *Poor Richard's
Almanack.* Of course, not all the
sayings here are original with old
Ben, for he included in *Poor
Richard*, along with his own,
proverbs copied or adapted from
other collections—but he usually
gave to them a flavor of his own.
The woodcuts are adapted from the
crude cuts of Joseph Crawhall.

With the old Almanack and the old Year,
Leave thy old Vices, tho' ever so dear.

Content makes poor Men rich;
Discontent makes rich Men poor.

If your head is wax, don't walk
in the Sun.

Fish and Visitors stink
after three days.

A country man between two lawyers,
is like a Fish between two Cats.

Well done is better than well said.

Who is rich? He that rejoices
in his Portion.

Half Wits talk much but say little.

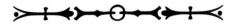

An open Foe may prove a curse;
But a pretended Friend is worse.

Wealth is not his that has it, but
his that enjoys it.

Wish not so much to live long,
as to live well.

Those who in Quarrels interpose,
Must often wipe a bloody nose.

Quarrels never could last long,
If on one side only lay the wrong.

What you would seem to be, be really.

Search others for their Virtues,
thyself for thy Vices.

Tart Words make no Friends:
a spoonful of honey will catch
more flies than a Gallon of Vinegar.

E'er you remark another's sin,
bid your own conscience look within.

To lengthen thy Life, lessen thy Meals.

He that cannot obey, cannot command.

Search others for their Virtues,
thyself for thy Vices.

Great beauty, great strength, and great
riches are really and truly of no great
use; a right Heart exceeds all.

Many complain of their Memory,
few of their Judgment.

To err is human, to repent divine;
to persist devilish.

He's a fool that makes his
Doctor his Heir.

He that lieth down with Dogs,
shall rise up with Fleas.

Beware of the young Doctor
and the old Barber.

Eat to live, and not live to eat.

God works wonders now and then;
Behold! a lawyer, an honest man.

The Honey is sweet,
but the Bee has a Sting.

Success has ruin'd many a Man.

Pran

God helps them that help themselves.

Pran

'Tis easier to suppress the first Desire,
than to satisfy all that follow it.

Pran

Work as if you were to live 100 years,
Pray as if you were to die To-morrow.

Pran

If you do what you should not,
you must hear what you would not.

Pran

If you'd have a servant that you like,
serve yourself.

Pran

For want of a Nail the Shoe is lost;
for want of a Shoe the Horse is lost;
for want of a Horse the Rider is lost.

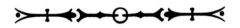

A little well-gotten will do us more good, than lordships and sceptres by Rapine and Blood.

Ill Customs and bad Advice are seldom forgotten.

He that speaks ill of the Mare, will buy her.

How few there are who have courage enough to own their Faults, or resolution enough to mend them!

The worst wheel of the cart makes the most noise.

He that would live in peace and at ease, must not speak all he knows, nor judge all he sees.

Who has deceiv'd thee so
oft as thy self?

A traveller should have a Hog's nose,
a Deer's legs, and an Ass's back.

An honest Man will receive neither
Money nor Praise that is not his due.

Avoid dishonest gain: no price
Can recompense the pangs of vice.

Many Foxes grow grey,
but few grow good.

Genius without Education
is like Silver in the Mine.

He that can travel well afoot,
keeps a good horse.

Doing an Injury puts you below your Enemy; Revenging one makes you but even with him; Forgiving it sets you above him.

A Pair of good Ears will wring dry an hundred Tongues.

Keep thy shop, and thy shop will keep thee.

Beware, beware; he'll cheat without scruple, who can without fear.

The poor Man must walk to get meat for his stomach, the rich man to get a stomach for his meat.

Avarice and Happiness never saw each other, how then should they become acquainted?

You can bear your own Faults,
why not a Fault in your Wife?

There's many witty Men whose brains
can't fill their bellies.

Let all Men know thee, but no man
know thee thoroughly: Men freely ford
that see the shallows.

Experience keeps a dear school,
yet Fools will learn in no other.

Industry pays Debts,
Despair increases them.

They who have nothing to trouble
them, will be troubled at nothing.

There is much difference between
imitating a good man, and
counterfeiting him.

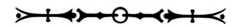

Be slow in chusing a Friend,
slower in changing.

'Tis easy to see, hard to foresee.

In a discreet man's mouth a publick
thing is private.

He that buys by the penny, maintains
not only himself, but other people.

Let thy maid-servant be faithful,
strong, and homely.

Here comes Courage! that seized
the Lion absent, and ran away from
the present Mouse.

He that hath a Trade, hath an Estate.

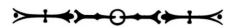

Where yet was ever found the mother,
who'd change her booby for another?

A ship under sail and a big-bellied
Woman, are the handsomest two things
that can be seen common.

Drive thy Business, or it will drive thee.

There are no fools so troublesome
as those that have wit.

Late Children, early Orphans.

You will be careful, if you are wise,
how you touch men's Religion,
or Credit, or Eyes.

Half-Hospitality opens his Door and
shuts up his Countenance.

Lend money to an Enemy, and thou'lt
gain him; to a Friend, and thou'lt
lose him.

The heart of the Fool is in his mouth,
but the mouth of the wise man
is in his heart.

Visit your Aunt, but not every Day;
and call at your Brother's,
but not every night.

Hear Reason, or she'll make
you feel her.

There are lazy Minds as well
as lazy Bodies.

An empty Bag cannot stand upright.

There's none deceived
but he that trusts.

Tricks and treachery are the practice
of Fools that have not wit enough
to be honest.

Little Strokes fell great Oaks.

Where there is Hunger, Law is not
regarded; and where Law is not
regarded, there will be Hunger.

***

The Way to see by Faith is to shut
the Eye of Reason.

***

The Morning Daylight appears plainer
when you put out your Candle.

***

The most exquisite Folly is made of
Wisdom spun too fine.

***

Clean your Finger,
before you point at my Spots.

***

Life with Fools consists in Drinking;
with the wise Man, living's Thinking.

At the working man's house Hunger
looks in, but dares not *enter*.

Who is strong? He that can conquer
his bad Habits.

Dine with little, sup with less:
Do better still; sleep supperless.

If you'd lose a troublesome Visitor,
lend him money.

The wise Man draws more Advantage
from his Enemies, than the Fool
from his Friends.

Each year one vicious habit rooted
out, in time might make the worst
man good throughout.

He that has not got a Wife, is not yet
a compleat Man.

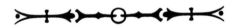

Fear to do ill, and you need
fear nought else.

Marry above thy match,
thou'lt get a master.

Promises may get thee friends,
but non-performance will turn
them into enemies.

Enjoy the present hour, be mindful of
the past; & neither fear nor wish the
approaches of the last.

Tho' Modesty is a Virtue,
Bashfulness is a Vice.

Hide not your Talents,
they for Use were made:
"What's a Sun-Dial in the Shade?"

If evils come not,
　　Then our fears are vain;
And if they do,
　　Fear but augments the pain.

Learn of the skillful:
He that teaches himself,
hath a fool for his master.

A man in a Passion rides a mad Horse.

Man's tongue is soft,
And bone doth lack;
Yet a stroke therewith
May break a man's back.

Fools make feasts and
Wise Men eat them.

The Creditors are a superstitious
sect, great observers of set
Days and Times.

Duty is not beneficial because it is
commanded, but is commanded
because it is beneficial.

Proclaim not all thou knowest,
ll thou owest, all thou hast,
nor all thou can'st.

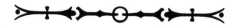

To bear other people's afflictions,
every one has courage and
enough to spare.

—◦—

Epitaph on a Scolding Wife
by her Husband: Here my poor
Bridget's Corps doth lie,
she is at rest,—and so am I.

—◦—

He's a Fool that cannot conceal
his Wisdom.

—◦—

All Blood is alike ancient.

—◦—

Tim was so learned, that he could
name a Horse in nine Languages.
So ignorant, that he bought
a Cow to ride on.

—◦—

A true Friend is the best Possession.

Great Spenders are bad Lenders.

You may talk too much on the
best of Subjects.

He who multiplies Riches
multiplies Cares.

The poor have little,
Beggars none;
The rich too much
Enough not one.

Let thy discontents be thy secrets;—
if the World knows them 'twill
despise thee and increase them.

Hear no ill of a Friend,
nor speak any of an Enemy.

Pay what you owe, and you'll know
what is your own.

An old man in a House is a good Sign.

Those who are fear'd, are hated.

At 20 years of age the will reigns;
at 30 the wit; at 40 the judgment.

If you would keep your secret from an
Enemy, tell it not to a Friend.

The Eye of a Master will do more
Work than his Hand.

The Traveller that is struck
by Lightning, seldom gets home
to tell his Widow.

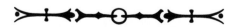

Beware of little Expenses:
a small leak will sink a great Ship.

There are no ugly loves,
nor handsome prisons.

He that would have a short Lent,
let him borrow money to be
repaid at Easter.

Eat few Suppers, and you'll need
few Medicines.

If Passion drives,
let Reason hold the Reins.

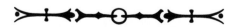

The Tongue offends,
and the Ears get the Cuffing.

Mankind are very odd Creatures:
One half censure what they practise,
the other half practise what
they censure; the rest always say
and do as they ought.

Grief often treads
Upon the heels of pleasure,
Marry'd in haste,
We oft repent at leisure;
Some by experience
Find these words misplaced,
Marry'd at leisure,
They repent in haste.

An undutiful Daughter will prove
an unmanageable Wife.

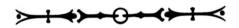

Glass, China, and Reputation, are
easily crack'd, and never well mended.

He is not well bred, that cannot bear
Ill-Breeding in others.

Kings and Bears often worry
their keepers.

Light Purse, heavy Heart.

A Brother may not be a Friend, but a
Friend will always be a Brother.

Ne'er take a Wife till thou hast a house
(and a fire) to put her in.

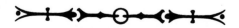

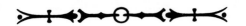

After three days men grow weary of a
wench, a guest, and weather rainy.

Plough deep while Sluggards sleep;
and you shall have Corn to sell
and to keep.

The proof of gold is fire;
the proof of woman, gold;
the proof of man, a woman.

Great talkers, little doers.

Take counsel in Wine,
but resolve afterwards in Water.

He that drinks fast, pays slow.

Wise Men learn by others' harms;
Fools by their own.

Wink at small faults—
remember thou hast great ones.

What maintains one Vice would bring
up two Children.

A quiet Conscience sleeps in Thunder,
but Rest and Guilt live far asunder.

He that won't be counsell'd,
can't be help'd.

Wink at small faults—
remember thou hast great ones.

Eat to please thyself, but dress to
please others.

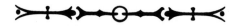

In Marriage without love, there will
be Love without Marriage.

Craft must be at charge for clothes,
but Truth can go naked.

Write Injuries in Dust,
Benefits in Marble.

Happy's the Wooing that's not
long a doing.

He that takes a Wife takes Care.

Lawyers, Preachers, and Tomtit's Eggs,
there are more of them hatched than
come to perfection.

Poverty wants some things,
Luxury many things,
Avarice all things.

FULLE !

A full Belly is the Mother of all Evil.

All things are cheap to the saving,
dear to the wasteful.

If you ride a Horse, sit close and tight
if you ride a Man, sit easy and light.

Would you persuade, speak of
interest, not of reason.

Serving God is doing good to Man,
but praying is thought an easier
Service, and therefore
more generally chosen.

What is Serving God?
'Tis doing Good to Man.

It is wise not to seek a Secret
and honest not to reveal it.

Samson, for all his strong Body,
had a weak Head, or he would not
have laid it in a Harlot's lap.

Ⲯ—◆—O—◆—Ⲯ

He that waits upon Fortune,
is never sure of a dinner.

Ⲯ—◆—O—◆—Ⲯ

Drink water, put the Money in your
pocket, and leave the dry-bellyache
in the punch-bowl.

Ⲯ—◆—O—◆—Ⲯ

Approve not of him who
commends all you say.

Ⲯ—◆—O—◆—Ⲯ

You cannot pluck roses
      Without fear of thorns,
Nor enjoy a fair wife
      Without danger of horns.

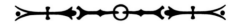

A Slip of the Foot you may soon
recover, but a slip of the Tongue
you may never get over.

Nothing humbler than Ambition,
when it is about to climb.

The discontented Man finds
no easy Chair.

Take heed of the Vinegar of sweet
Wine, and the Anger of Good-nature.

The Bell calls others to Church,
but itself never minds the Sermon.

You may delay, but Time will not.

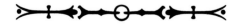

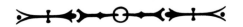

Have you somewhat to do tomorrow,
do it today.

Neither a Fortress nor a Maidenhead
will hold out long after they
begin to parley.

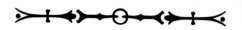

The good or ill hap of a good or ill
Life, is the good or ill choice of a
good or ill Wife.

What one relishes, nourishes.

All things are easy to Industry,
all things difficult to Sloth.

A house without woman and firelight,
is like a Body without soul or sprite.

Teach your Child to hold his tongue,
he'll learn fast enough to speak.

In Rivers and bad Governments, the
lightest things swim at top.

Cut the Wings of your Hens and
Hopes, lest they lead you a weary
Dance after them.

Would you live with ease, do what you
ought, not what you please.

The Horse thinks one thing, and he
that saddles him another.

Love your Neighbor;
yet don't pull down your Hedge.

When Prosperity was well mounted,
she let go the Bridle and soon came
tumbling out of the Saddle.

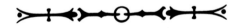

In the Affairs of this World Men
are saved, not by Faith,
but by the Want of it.

Friendship cannot live with Ceremony,
nor without Civility.

A good Wife lost, is God's gift lost.

He is ill clothed that is bare of Virtue.

Men and melons are hard to know.

He's the best physician that knows
the worthlessness of most medicines.

Keep your Mouth wet, Feet dry.

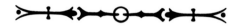

If you would reap Praise
you must sow the Seeds,
gentle Words and useful Deeds.

Early to Bed and early to rise, makes a
Man healthy, wealthy, and wise.

An old young man will be a
young old man.

Sudden Pow'r is apt to be insolent,
sudden Liberty saucy; that behaves
best which has grown gradually.

Many have quarrel'd about Religion,
that never practised it.

The thrifty maxim of the wary Dutch, is
to save all the money they can touch.

It is better to take many Injuries,
than to give one.

Trust thyself, and another
shall not betray thee.

Haste makes Waste.

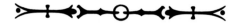

Diligence is the mother of good luck.

Do not do that which you would
not have known.

God heals and the doctor takes the fee.

If thou would'st live long, live well; for
Folly and Wickedness shorten life.

He that pays for work before it's done,
has but a pennyworth for two pence.

You may be more happy than Princes,
if you will be more virtuous.

Thou can'st not joke an Enemy
into a Friend, but thou may'st a Friend
into an Enemy.

Anger is never without a Reason,
but seldom with a good One.

Eating sour Pickles won't kill
your Appetite.

An ill Wound, but not an ill Name,
may be healed.

Many Dishes, many Diseases.

Wish a Miser long life,
and you wish him no good.

God, Parents, and Instructors,
can never be requited.

The Sting of a Reproach
is the Truth of it.

Drink does not drown Care,
but waters it, and makes it grow faster.

Three may keep a secret if two
of them are dead.

━━◦━━

He that resolves to mend hereafter,
resolves not to mend now.

━━◦━━

When the well's dry,
we know the worth of water.

━━◦━━

A quarrelsome Man has no
good Neighbours.

━━◦━━

Many a Man would have been worse, if
his Estate had been better.

━━◦━━

If you would not be forgotten,
as soon as you are dead and rotten,
either write things worth reading,
or do things worth the writing.

Sell not virtue to purchase wealth, nor liberty to purchase power.

Keep your eyes wide open before Marriage, half shut afterwards.

Why does the blind man's Wife paint herself?

Creditors have better memories than Debtors.

Forewarn'd, forearm'd.

Many a Man thinks he is buying Pleasure, when he is really selling himself a Slave to it.

Time is an herb that cures all diseases.

Great Talkers should be cropp'd,
for they have no need of Ears.

There is no Man so bad but he
secretly respects the Good.

⊱┈❀┈⊰

Pray don't burn my House
to roast your Eggs.

⊱┈❀┈⊰

Since thou art not sure of a Minute,
throw not away an Hour.

⊱┈❀┈⊰

As we must account for every
idle Word, so we must for
every idle Silence.

⊱┈❀┈⊰

He that can have Patience can
have what he will.

⊱┈❀┈⊰

Good wives and good plantations are
made by good Husbands.

He that scatters thorns,
let him not go barefoot.

Drunkenness, that worst of Evils,
makes some men Fools,
some Beasts, some Devils.

Most People return small Favours,
acknowledge middling ones, and repay
great ones with Ingratitude.

Don't judge of Men's Wealth or Piety,
by their Sunday Appearances.

The Golden Age never was
the present Age.

Is there anything men take
more pains about than to make
themselves unhappy?

To whom thy secret thou dost tell, to
him thy freedom thou dost sell.

Meanness is the Parent of Insolence.

The sleeping Fox catches no poultry.
Up! Up!

Write with the learned, pronounce
with the vulgar.

An egg to-day is better than a
hen to-morrow.

Tell a miser he's rich, and woman she's
old, you'll get no Money of one, nor
Kindness of t'other.

The Proud hate Pride—in others.

Men, dally not with other Folks'
Women or Money.

The rotten Apple spoils
his Companion.

Friendship increases by visiting
Friends, but by visiting seldom.

Cunning proceeds from
Want of Capacity.

What more valuable than Gold?
Diamonds. Than Diamonds? Virtue.

'Tis great Confidence in a Friend
to tell him your Faults,
greater to tell him his.

Great Estates may venture more;
Little Boats must keep near Shore.

You may be too cunning for one,
but not for all.

'Tis easier to prevent bad Habits
than to break them.

'Tis easier to prevent bad Habits
than to break them.

Let thy Child's first lesson be
obedience, and the second
will be what thou wilt.

Blessed is he that expects nothing
for he shall never be disappointed.

Be at War with your Vices, at Peace
with your Neighbours, and let every
New-Year find you a better Man.

Nothing dries sooner than a Tear.

A Change of Fortune hurts a wise man
no more than a Change of the Moon.

When Knaves betray each other,
one can scarce be blamed or the
other pitied.

Fools need Advice most, but only wise
Men are the better for it.

Silence is not always a Sign of
Wisdom, but Babbling is ever a Folly.

For Age and Want save while you may;
No morning Sun lasts a whole Day.

He that hath no Ill-Fortune
will be troubled with Good.

Where Sense is wanting,
Everything is wanting.

Two dry Sticks will burn a green One.

Little Rogues easily become
great Ones.

He is a Governor that governs
his Passions, and he a Servant
that serves them.

You may sometimes be much
in the Wrong, in owning your
being in the Right.

He that's content hath enough.
He that complains has too much.

Old Boys have their Playthings as
well as young Ones; the Difference
is only in the Price.

The family of fools is ancient.

Half Wits talk much but say little

Virtue may not always make a
Face handsome, but Vice will
certainly make it ugly.

When man and woman die,
as poets sung
His heart's the last part moves,
Her last, the tongue.

What you seem to be, be really.

The Things which hurt, instruct.

No Gains without Pains.

If man could have Half his Wishes
he would double his troubles.

Don't throw stones at your
neighbours', if your own
Windows are glass.

He that riseth late, must trot all day,
and shall scarce overtake
his business at night.

He that can compose himself, is wiser
than he that can compose books.

After crosses and losses,
men grow humbler and wiser.

No better relation than a prudent
and faithful friend.

There are three faithful friends—
an old Wife, an old Dog,
and ready Money.

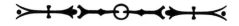

Industry, Perserverance, & Frugality,
make Fortune yield.

O Lazy bones! Dost thou think
God would have given thee arms and
legs, if He had not design'd thou
should'st use them?

Be always ashamed to catch
thyself idle.

Here comes Glib-Tongue:
who can out-flatter a dedication;
and lie, like ten Epitaphs.

Virtue and a Trade,
are a Child's best Portion.

Field well till'd and a little Wife
well will'd, are great riches.

Don't think to hunt two Hares
with one Dog.

Do good to thy friend to keep him,
to thy enemy to gain him.

To be humble to superiors is duty;
to equals courtesy,
to inferiors nobleness.

Declaiming against Pride, is not always
a Sign of Humility.

Observe all men, thyself most.

Если you have time, don't wait for Time.

When you speak to a man,
look on his eyes, when he speaks
to thee, look on his mouth.

As Pride increases, Fortune declines

Prayers and Provender
hinder no journey.

Fear not Death;
for the sooner we die,
the longer shall we be immortal.

Death takes no Bribes.